T0095699

The Exchange

Wild Times and Italian Rhymes

iUniverse

THE EXCHANGE
WILD TIMES AND ITALIAN RHYMES

iUniverse books may be ordered through booksellers or by contacting:

iUniverse
1663 Liberty Drive
Bloomington, IN 47403
www.iuniverse.com
1-800-Authors (1-800-288-4677)

ISBN: 978-1-4917-9118-9 (sc)
ISBN: 978-1-4917-9119-6 (e)

Library of Congress Control Number: 2016903396

Print information available on the last page.

iUniverse rev. date: 2/26/2016

To all those people who always believed in me and the heights that I could reach. You all will be in my heart. The time we have spent together has made life worthwhile.

Contents

I

The Exchange: Wild Times and Italian Rhymes

Author Disclaimer: Everything in this book represents events that happened from the perspective of the author and are opinions from Jesse Mata, whom the story is about. These opinions are presented as nothing more than personal beliefs and feelings; they are his and his alone. None of the opinions mentioned in this book are endorsed by the publishing company, editors, agents, representatives, or others who worked on this project. This is a story about a brief time in the life of the Jesse Mata, and that is why names of people and places have been changed. Certain people have been left out of this book to protect their anonymity and privacy. Jesse Mata and author Jessy King, personally and in business respectively, understand that everyone has individual beliefs and views of what happened long ago. As an author, Jessy King deserves the respect and opportunity to tell things from his point of view.

Thank you kindly,

Jessy King

Introduction
(introduzione)

When an accident happens, we, as people, tend to take credit for having some sort of control over the accident if it works out; but when something happens that doesn't go as planned, we are quick to say it was just an accident and try to distance ourselves as soon as we can and move on. Well, what if a series of accidents and things that are out of one's control keep happening? Is it fate pushing that person in a direction, or is it just the luck of the draw and said person should just roll with the punches? Even after everything that has happened in my life, I have no answer to that question. What I do know is that whether it was fate or just another boring collection of happenstances, I had an amazing, heartrending, and downright life-changing experience.

My adventure began back in the spring of 2001, when I was approached by an adviser of the high school I was attending at the time. It was my junior year, and I had academic progress reports and scheduling for the following year, as well as college preparatory tests and classes. After my evaluation, my adviser realized that by fall of 2001 I would be done with all my high school credits and I had a few choices: I could finish early and wait for graduation in spring, volunteer in local middle schools or outdoor schooling (both of which I briefly did, and I couldn't stand teaching), or look into high school exchange for my senior year of high school. I took a long look at all my options, and I was invited to an exchange student return dinner to see whether this was something I would want to do.

With so much to think about and my home life not being exactly the best at the time, anything that would put me farther away from home would be better. I had to think about possibly attending community college classes, getting a job, moving to the big city (if you can call Portland, Oregon, a big city), or heading out of the country. I flew back to Omaha that summer to talk to the rest of my family about the possibility of leaving the country for my senior year of high school. None of my relatives really gave me any good advice, and most of them advised against it. They said it would be expensive and there was no point; they told me to just go to college and hope for the best. Finally, one specific conversation with my grandma made me realize I could be missing out on something great. My grandma had lived in Europe about forty years earlier, so she was the one voice I listened to, simply because she had done something no one else in my family had. I figured I had no reason not to take advice from the adventurous woman I had come to admire.

When I returned to Oregon in late summer of 2001, my father and I had a long talk about why I needed to do this. With financial help, scholarships, and family contributions, we started the process. It took about five months of hard prep work that needed to be done. We were organized and diligent, and soon I was all set. There were meetings, counseling sessions, and orientations galore. If my memory serves me right, I believe I went to a total of thirty-five exchange-program meetings, events, and appointments to make sure I had all the proper paperwork and student work visas to live in another country. In all these events, there was an emphasis on how students change; they become different and better people.

I never really understood the personal-growth aspect of things, simply because nothing in my life up to that point had really made me want to be better or change for any grand purpose (and nothing has done so to this day). I just felt this was one more thing to do before I went to college, got a job, and lived in small-town bliss with no change to me or the world around me. I have noticed that people who have grand dreams have to be very connected with those dreams to make them come true. For the rest of us, we have to try things and hope something works out. That's not to discourage putting effort into everyday life; it just means that there are two paths in life: contented with life or discontented with no hope. So I found it amusing to listen to some of the returning exchange students claim huge life changes and then see these same people at a university going for a degree with the hopes of getting a $30,000-a-year job. (For the record, $30,000 was a lot of money back in 2001.) That is not to put down those people and all the changes they went through; it's just hard for me to see someone change that much as a seventeen-year-old and then, less than a year later, this "mature, changed person" is doing body shots off a cheerleader at a college mixer. (Not that I know about any underage drinking and sorority or fraternity parties; to the best of my recollection, I never drank anything but root beer.)

When I returned to high school for the beginning of fall term in September 2001, I was ready to be done with high school, head off to Europe, and begin something new. Well, just about seven or eight days into my senior year, the September 11 terrorist attacks on the World Trade Center happened. I had already been nervous about leaving, and now I had to worry about anti-American sentiment and terrorists. In my view, they were never terrorists but rather criminals who got lucky with a few attacks. (Adolf Hitler, in my view, was a terrorist; Osama bin Laden was just another criminal.) So after this new world event, I went back into exchange-program damage-control mode and more meetings about safety and who to contact while overseas.

As fall term drew to a close, I began packing for my trip. I had everything ready so that after winter break I could just get on a plane and fly away. When I came back from winter break, I got a ticket to fly to San Francisco for my first stop, where I would meet up with all the West Coast students before we went on to New York to meet up with the rest of the Americans going to Europe and Russia. When I got to the airport, I was stopped by a news crew asking people entering the airport how we felt about the new security measures. I don't remember saying anything important, as I was so distracted with the tasks that had been laid in front of me. So with my bags packed, and after one final hug from my dad, away I went.

CHAPTER 1

How This All Got Started
(come tutto questo è cominciato)

With most exchange programs, you have about a half a year to decide what country you will go to, how much the cost will be, academic prerequisites, and so forth. Well, since I got a scholarship to pay part of my costs and my high school credits had been fulfilled, my only choice was where I wanted to go. I chose three countries: Spain, France, and Italy. I felt Spain would be the best choice, because I spoke a little Spanish and my family was from Spain. Out of random coincidence, I had my spot to Spain taken away because some girl in California decided she wanted to go and took the spot she had given up originally (at least that is the story that was told to me). So my exchange-program adviser began the paperwork so I could go to France. What happened with my application for France I never found out, but there was one spot left for Italy, so I took it. My mother's family is from Sicily, so I figured it would be nice to see Italy and where my family came from.

The terror attacks on September 11 had had a huge impact on how everyone acted since then, but this never discouraged me one bit. I had the view that if something happened, well, I guess it was meant to be. (In Italian, this is put as *era destinato.*) I kept hearing the phrase "Meant to be" a lot while I was traveling. I think people sometimes try to give fate a prominent role in order to feel more connected to their sometimes uneventful lives. That way when something amazing happens, they can claim all the mundane work they did was for a greater purpose. Sorry for being cynical, but let's leave romance and whimsy for fiction books.

When the terror attacks of September 11 happened, I was actually still asleep. It was around six o'clock in the morning on the West Coast of the United States. I actually didn't even know where the World Trade Center towers were. I thought they were attacking Seattle (I was confusing the World Trade Center with the World Trade Organization). I don't remember doing much that day; a friend of mine at school had a radio, and we sat in the quad of the school and just listened for what seemed like hours. It was so odd to think we were under attack. Sometimes it doesn't feel real, but I remember what I saw when I was in New York City in the winter of 2001/2. When I was there, the severely damaged South Tower of the World Trade

Center was still there, covered in snow. I can't get that image out of my head. It looked like a movie set, but the smell of burnt metal and rotting buildings was still there. Even in winter and under snow, the sights, sounds, and smells were shocking. Even as I write this, it haunts my memory; this is something no person should ever have to remember. I haven't been to New York City since, and I haven't really needed or wanted to go. I'm sure everything is different now, but I just can't get those images out of my brain.

So, after less than a week in New York, my exchange group was ready for the long flight to Frankfurt, Germany. From Germany we would go on to our individual countries. It was a red-eye flight, and I sat next to a girl who was from Wisconsin. We talked for most of the night and slept the rest of the way. After we made it to Germany, we had some down time before my smaller group had to head off to Rome to meet up with all the exchange students from all over the world. I never saw anything outside the Frankfurt airport, but there sure were a lot of blonde-haired, blue-eyed people in Germany. I was really taken aback at how many people flowed in and out of European airports, speaking many different languages.

I got a flight to the famous Leonardo da Vinci International Airport in Rome. My group got on a charter bus, and at that point I had been traveling about sixteen hours with flights and transfers. All I wanted to do was get to the villa we would be staying in and sleep. We got to the villa, and all I remember is going straight to bed, even though I could smell the amazing food downstairs. For about a half a week, we stayed at a villa retreat with people from all over the world. My roommates were two guys from Chicago and a guy from New Zealand. It was amazingly beautiful. It wasn't cold in central Italy; it was like the weather in Los Angeles.

After a couple days of rest, we had more orientation meetings and some team-building exercises, though I can't remember the purpose of any of it. Regardless, we were all away from home and loving it. During some of our down time, we got to talk to others who were there. I met this girl who was from the outback of Australia; she was half Irish and half aboriginal, and I had never in my life seen a girl as beautiful as she was. All that plus her amazing Australian accent made a perfect package. I spent most, if not all, of my time with her while we were in Rome. I never saw her again after that week; my program was longer than hers, and we lost contact over time—mostly because I didn't have a cell phone back then and I didn't check e-mail very often.

The morning of what I thought was about halfway through January, I got on a train headed for Taranto, Italy. It is a little bay town inside the heel of the boot on the Italian peninsula. The train ride took about four hours, and I think I took three or maybe four different trains to get there. After the long trip, there were about fifteen or sixteen people, including my host family, who came to pick me up. Everyone was excitedly hugging me and speaking really quickly; I'm not affectionate at all, so this was weird for me. Several people spoke English, so it was easy for me to follow what was happening and what my new family was saying. After all the introductions, I got in the car with my host family. They began speaking quickly, as if there were tons of things to do now that I was there.

I got back to the family's condo and took the longest bath I have ever taken, washing off days of travel and exhaustion. I remember just eating, sleeping, and sitting on the veranda for the first three days, trying to acclimate to my new home. Everywhere we went, the food, sights, sounds, and smells were heavenly.

CHAPTER 2

Off to School
(a scuola)

The next week, I started taking classes at an Italian art school called a Liceo Artistico, which is just a high school for art and media students. On the first day of all my classes, people had hundreds of questions for me. From what little Spanish I could speak, I could understand some things, but other than that I had to rely on people speaking what little English they could. For the first month I was there, I had to speak Spanish, because that was the only way I could get locals to understand what I was trying to say. I had people write down on a notepad how to say things in Italian so I could get from one place to another, since most of the time I was by myself while going to and from school. Luckily Spanish, French, and Italian are similar, so I was able to get pretty far. I could go shopping, eat out, and get on the right buses and trains. School was still a place for me to connect and really try to understand all my basics.

One thing did shake me a little. About halfway through my first month in Italy, I was being driven to school by my host mother, who didn't work too far from the school and wanted me to get used to the route I would be taking to school every day, in case I needed to walk. On our way home later that same day, a car ran through a very busy intersection and hit the driver's side of the car. I, my host brother, and my host mother were hit so hard I don't remember much after that. It was so random and out of the blue. All I remember is people yelling in Italian until the police and tow trucks arrived. We all walked home that night, not in too much pain. That was the last time until Easter I rode in a car with anyone from my host family.

I mostly stuck to public transportation. After my first month was over and I was getting used to public transportation, one Saturday night after a long day at school (my art school classes were six days a week from 8:00 a.m. to 1:00 p.m.), I had met some people from school downtown, and later my host family also came downtown. One of my host brothers and I wanted to stay out later with my new friend Julie, who was from Denmark, and some other kids from school, so we took the bus home. After the bus left the downtown area and was ready to get onto the main thoroughfare, we were hit from out of nowhere by a guy driving way over the speed limit who drove almost under the bus. A night of winding down turned into a witness lineup for police until they figured out what had happened. After that I walked everywhere I went for about three weeks. I couldn't handle being in vehicles for a while.

During the second month, I started taking private Italian lessons from one of the former exchange program hosts. Over time I started substituting Italian words and phrases for the Spanish I was speaking, and by the end of the second month I could speak basic Italian and Tarantino, the local dialect where I lived. I guess the good thing about having to learn a language quickly for survival is that it really makes you think about what you want to say—no fluff, no filler; just say it. Most people didn't have time to sit and wait to try to figure out what I wanted; they just would move on if I couldn't get it. It's a real shot to the ego being a fully functioning human being and feeling helpless in a foreign land, but what else was I going to do.

I bought a calling card one day, and from that day on I spent a lot of time calling back home and talking to relatives just to hear people speaking English again. My host family was interested in some things about where I lived and where I was from, but most of the time they went about their own business and left me alone. That is why I am forever indebted to my two best friends for life, Julie from Denmark and Kristine from Norway, who became my global sisters. I met both about a week apart. I met Julie first, because she lived in the same town I was in and went to the same school. We both spoke English, which was a relief to us because we both were learning Italian. Kristine and I met along with Julie at some function for exchange students, and so the trio was complete. We all hit it off immediately and were inseparable the entire time we were there. We shared secrets, went to the beach, laughed at our crazy host families, and talked about who liked who at school and all kinds of gossip on any particular day. We also cried together when things were not going well. We made special trips and went out of our ways to see each other, even if it was for just an hour. Kristine was one town over, so most of the school days saw just Julie and me together. Julie was living with the woman who was in charge of our exchange program, because her original host family had bailed after treating her more like a maid than a guest. I met her old host family one time when we had to go pick up the rest of Julie's stuff, and I had never seen such downright mafioso behavior and weirdness in my whole life.

There was other stuff that had happened, but I never got up the courage to ask. I could tell Julie had gone through a lot of mental and physical hardship, but I just wanted a friend, so we left any talk of bad things alone and went on with our fun.

Regarding Kristine, I never knew anything about her host family; they were more or less nonexistent. I think she had the best family out of all of us. I found out after the fact that two months into my stay in Italy, my family was trying to have me transferred to a different family because I was not a fit, as they saw it. They would mostly speak English when I was around, but whenever they wanted to complain about me, they spoke Italian. Italian curse words are very similar to French and Spanish curse words, however, so I knew what they were calling me; I just didn't let them know that. I had to have weekly talks about my attitude and behavior and what kind of person I wanted to be while I was in Italy and whether it was going to make my host family look bad. I was told on a regular basis that I needed to be better at every aspect of my life, and now that I was away from my family, I was going to get proper education on how to be a better person from a bunch of self-absorbed, whiny know-it-alls. In hindsight, I can see why some of the things they did may have been beneficial, but I never listened, and I never understood the personal attacks or what made me such a bad person that they needed to point out every flaw I had; in fact, most of the perceived flaws were because of where I came from. That is why I spent so much time away from the house; I just didn't want to hear my daily list of shortcomings. I was constantly reminded that I was a guest—*not* a family member but a *guest*. My days at the house mostly consisted of chores or reading.

After the family realized that I was more of a popular attraction than their own kids, they made it a point to not invite me very many places. The exchange-program director saw this and came up with a great idea to fix my situation. If the family didn't want me around, then the program director was going to send me out to work—because why deal with the problems at hand when we can run away from them?

CHAPTER 3

Traveling Speaker
(diffusore in viaggio)

At the beginning of March, I was offered a position as a teacher's assistant in about three different local classrooms and then went on to travel to other cities across Italy and work in classrooms. That was the first time I felt truly useful while there. I was a guest speaker in English, history, and politics classes, and I loved it. While I wasn't a huge fan of the teaching part, it was great to get to talk about life, politics, and being a foreigner in a foreign land. I can't even remember how many cities and classrooms I visited, how many field trips I went on, and how much sightseeing I did.

I was hosted by many families over the three months I traveled. I got to taste all kinds of wines, cheeses, and every kind of meat and pasta. The families I stayed with were nice, but still everyone was standoffish. It is very hard to take a stranger into your home and feel completely comfortable, even if it is for a good cause. I guess I didn't notice until years later how odd it must have been for those families to have a foreign stranger living among them. While traveling, I saw all of Venice and St. Mark's cathedral, I saw Rome, Vatican City, Pope John Paul II, Naples, and many small towns and villages.

One story sticks out in my mind from my time in Venice, but the exact date in March has slipped away from me. I was invited to talk at a political science and history class. They happened to be studying a small chapter on American history and politics, and I was part of a two-day discussion with this class. About two or three minutes into my speech, a guy in the back wanted to ask a question. I permitted him to ask me, via translation through the teacher so I could understand the question easier. The guy in the back of the room asked me if, as an American, I was embarrassed that President George W. Bush was my country's leader. I was completely taken aback. I knew this was a question I could not answer easily. Even though my family members were not fans of George Bush or the Bush family, I had to answer the question delicately. See, if I acted offended, then I would have been playing the verbose and tell-me-no-wrong American; but if I acted blasé, I would have been a traitor to my culture. I explained to the whole class that I was not old enough to vote, so my personal preference didn't matter politically. However, I explained I was an old-fashioned Midwest Democrat and that President Bush didn't believe what I believed. I then segued into a discussion about my home state and explained that America was very different from how the rest of the world sees it. I explained that although American was my nationality, Nebraska and Oregon had shaped who I was. I know the question was meant to bait to me and catch me off guard, but I just spoke from the heart and had the teacher translate. By the end of class that day, I had them all eating out of the palm of my hand. There is one thing that always crosses all cultures—humor. No one should ever forget the power that comes from getting people to laugh at our commonalities and differences.

On one of my travel dates, I met up with a girl from Chile who was my speaking partner that week, and she had a great idea for out last night in Venice. She wanted to go to an Italian nightclub. By the time I got into the club, she was dancing on tables. She got kicked out twice, threw up in the parking lot, and dragged me to another club, and somehow we still got up early the next day, went to church with hangovers, and caught our train for our next teaching assignment. We ran into a bunch of other exchange students that we had met over our time there; it was a party that would not end.

Even though the night scenes were amazing, and the art, museums, and churches were beautiful and breathtaking, and everything we did was a blast, it was certainly nothing compared to the beaches—soft white-sand beaches all over the southern part of Italy. It still feels like a dream sometimes. I mean, don't get me wrong; the Alps were spectacular—but the sun and the sand were great. In southern Italy, we would buy some panini after school and go lie on the beach. It was great sunbathing, and it was hot but never unbearable. I am from Nebraska, a land of snowdrifts and tornadoes; give me a warm beach any day of the week.

While I was riding the rails, it was nice. I had a lot of time to think, look through photos I had taken, and write in my journal. Although Venice was amazingly beautiful, Rome took the cake for me. From Vatican City to the Colosseum and from the Piazza Spanglio to Fountain of Trevi, there was no place that wasn't captivating. During a trip I made to Rome on Easter weekend, I saw Pope John Paul II. He could speak pretty well and was mobile, going around the city of Rome. I am Catholic, but at no point during any of my tour of Rome or Vatican City did I have some huge Catholic reawakening. I actually had the opposite feeling. Seeing the pope is like seeing Elvis in concert. Yeah, there are other good concerts, but once you have seen the King, nothing else compares, right? The only feeling I had was a very creepy, eerie feeling when I was in the Colosseum. The idea that three thousand years ago Christians were fed to animals and gladiators fought there seemed so surreal and odd to me. It was hard to image how far we have come with technology but not in mind-set. It was just crazy, simply because so much history had happened inside St. Peter's Basilica and Rome, but the Colosseum and the ruins of the great Roman Empire standing over the Roman people always gave me chills. Just the idea that I was standing where warriors gathered, slaves were sold, and vestal virgins were presented before the emperors of Rome unnerved me. I don't know if that makes me a bad Catholic for not getting more out my religious history or if I am just a history nerd and I can't get enough of the ancient world and my Roman pagan roots. I do have to say, in benefit to the basilica, that St. Peter's tomb is a sight to be seen. Even if you don't believe the folklore, the tomb is amazing. And I understand that not everyone is fan of Pope John Paul II, but I have to give the man credit—he was very articulate and had a great presence about him when he spoke.

There were other things about Rome that captivated me as well: the balcony where Mussolini was hauled down and dragged through the streets, Liberty Square, and Castello St. Angelo, where some of the great kings and queens of Europe married over the centuries. By far my favorite moment during my weekend in Rome was when my host brothers and I had been traveling together and, on Saturday during Holy Week, just before Easter, we stopped for lunch at the Fountain of Trevi, and huge amounts of people from all over came and took pictures and tossed coins into the fountain in hopes of returning to

Rome someday. Before we left, I asked what the legend was regarding throwing a coin into the fountain. I was told I had to stand with my back to the fountain and throw the coin over my shoulder; with good luck, someday I would return to Rome. The only coin I had in my pocket was a penny from the US, so I tossed it in. Since I didn't have any more American money, every time I went to Rome after that, I would throw in a euro coin.

The last thing I had to do before I left the eternal city was having a cappuccino from a café in Rome. Since I was a visitor, I asked the barista what he would recommend. He told me to order a *doppio cappuccino a secco*, which roughly means "double cappuccino dry," meaning very little milk, a double shot of espresso, and lots of foam. That's the way the Romans drink it. So with my camera full, my taste buds satisfied, and my eyes filled with everything Italy and southern Austria had to offer, I would periodically return back to my home base to check in and take more art classes.

While I traveled, I couldn't stop taking pictures and writing in my journal, and when I was in those classrooms, I would paint pictures of what I had seen. No matter how much I tried to focus inside the classrooms, even the ones I was teaching in, my mind seemed to wander to the many outdoor and indoor splendors I had seen, as well as those I still wanted to see.

CHAPTER 4

Manduria
(la citta di Manduria)

At the end of May, I was offered a chance to go speak to a class in the town just a few kilometers away from where I was living. It was the hometown of my host mother, so I got the chance to stay at my host grandmother's villa in a small town named Manduria. It was a quaint little village, with churches everywhere. Since I had to teach only one day, that left about three days of free time for my host grandmother to teach me how to cook some the best food I have eaten in my life to this day. She spoke Italian but mostly spoke a dialect that I didn't completely understand. But the one thing I understood was that if we wanted to eat, we were going to have to make things from scratch. It was like watching a chef, and she wanted me to mimic everything she was doing so we could see whose tomato sauce would come out the best. Mine was good, but her sauce was phenomenal. I couldn't believe she took all those things from her garden and cupboard, and turned them into the best dish of sauce and pasta I had ever had.

It was like an art project. I always admired that lunch and dinner were these big productions, but I thought it was amazing that people took the time to make good food and enjoy it. It made the rest of each day worth it. To prepare great food, set a great table, and eat well, and then to end it all with an afternoon nap—all I can say is *wow.* When I woke up feeling refreshed, just in time for my afternoon coffee, I was ready for the next part of my day. What a way to live. To enjoy the small and simple things of life was refreshing.

It was my host grandmother that helped me to cook and eat things I had thought I would never try. It was in Manduria that I tasted escargot and goulash made from bull and horse meat (yes, I said horse meat). It all tasted so great I would forget what is was and just enjoy the meals. Don't get me wrong—the pizza in Italy is great, plain and simple; the pasta is out of this world; the bread … I can't even begin to tell you; and then there were hundreds of kinds of gelato that would make children scream for more ice cream. But trying all the foods that seemed exotic to me was an eye-opening experience.

What I was not expecting about Manduria was sightseeing there. I thought all the sights to see were in the big cities, but I was heavily mistaken. On one of the days I was in Manduria, I visited a mass grave from old

Greco–Roman conflicts. I was told that over the centuries thousands, and possibly even millions, had been buried in the desert, as it is easy to bury people in sand. To this day I still have a piece of an ancient vase that was given to me. Walking through the hallowed ground was crazy, as most of the graves had been excavated because of erosion and thousands of years of natural and man-made disasters, but still the sense of hallowedness was the same.

The last day I was in Manduria, me and my whole host family were invited to dinner at a family friend's house. After the meal, the host asked me if there was anything I would like see or do before I left their village, and I said I would just love to walk around town and take pictures, and after wandering around, the man asked me if I wanted to see an old Jewish ghetto from back during World War II. I was hesitant about going in, knowing the gravity of the war, but when I got inside, I couldn't believe how small everything was and that there was only one well and no running water in the whole ghetto. They had one garden for all the people living inside. It was beautiful in a way, but it was also sad to think those people had to be forced into those little ghettos simply to comply with wartime treaties was heartbreaking. It was a surprise and privilege to see history in person. And the most amazing thing about the ghetto was the people who still lived there had no grudges about what had been done; they were positive about the future. This is a lesson we should all keep close to the vest.

CHAPTER 5

Confusion
(confuzione)

As time passed and spring turned into summer, I found myself thinking a lot about my stay in Italy as a whole, knowing that by the beginning of May I had only two months left. It was strange to think that no matter where I was in the world, all my problems and lifetime shortcomings came along with me. I remember spending many nights crying on the phone with my great-grandmother when I was feeling down about school, living with a family that didn't care for me and didn't want me there, failed teen romances, and why I felt so crazy. I remember asking her one night what made me different from all the rest of my friends and family that just hung back in Omaha with jobs, families, homes, and other responsibilities. My great-grandmother told me that sometimes it's the craziest, most adventurous people who end up making the differences in the world around them. I didn't realize how important those phone calls would be.

About twenty days after returning to the United States, my great-grandmother would pass away, and my great-grandfather would pass on three months to the day after her. I took my great-grandparents' advice because they had so much to do with my growing up. I guess when I was in Italy I felt they were the only two people in the whole world I could tell my life's trials and tribulations to without any judgment. Thinking back now, it was that year, 2002, in which I completely checked out of reality. Returning from Europe and trying to readjust to reality was tough enough, and after my great-grandparents died, it was terrible, because I couldn't image being loved, comforted, or so important to anyone else on this planet. Being alone in Europe was a trial in my life. I would never go back and change anything that happened or anything I said or did, even if I could. I collected much strength in my weaker moments, so if I needed to break down, I could, and I could talk to the two people who really wanted me and wanted to know my joys, my hurts, and my every thought, even if such a thought was "I had the best pizza of my life today."

When you are young, you believe life moves in mundane smoothness. As you get older, you come to know life is much bumpier. My great-grandparents were so proud that I went on this adventure that it didn't matter how betrayed I was by people who called me a friend and then left when things got tough. I never blinked an eye when my family was so quick to judge my struggles with "I told you so" rather than understanding. A bad grade in school? I didn't try hard enough. Got lost in town or didn't make an appointment? It was my laziness. Couldn't understand something? Well, I needed to get better at Italian, as no one would wait for me. Amid all the stress and pressure, I saw very few people doing anything to better their lives, but they had time to judge me. I don't know many people I grew up with who could do what I did. My Catholicism would never once let me talk back without punishment. I was never mean or disrespectful, even though most the time I was left out, made fun of, and downright verbally abused because I was not perfect, as my host family claimed to be. And could I ever get any sympathy from my own family, back home? Never. I always had to remember I was the one who chose to be in the situation, and I would hear the "We never got these chances, and you don't know how hard we worked to get you where you are" speech. (For the record, my parents worked very hard, and my sister and I are much better off in life because of the things they gave up so we could have more.)

As I write this down, it is still hard for me to say these things about people who opened their home to me and fed me, but the way they and the exchange program treated me was just plain wrong. Whenever I brought up a concern or problem, I was blamed for the causing the problem. I remember one night when my host family, for whatever reason, told me I had to be home at 8:00 p.m., though they knew a mandatory function I had to attend would not start until seven thirty that evening. My host mother and father told me I had to choose loyalty to either them or the exchange-program leaders (who were supposedly corrupting what the family felt was their good instruction). Of course the function didn't end until close to eleven that night. Well, the family would not open the gate to the apartment complex, because I had disobeyed them. So I spent about three days at the exchange-program leader's house with no clothes to change into or any school supplies or anything. After the family realized they would not get their stipend check for the next month if they didn't change their behavior, they let me back in. After that incident, they never made it a point to tell me when dinner was, and more often than not I would eat in town before I went home, because I knew there would be no dinner. I got to eat lunch, but the family would all head to their rooms when I got home, and so I would stay out as late as I could, so they could have time with each other without me being around.

I spent much of my time during my last two months in the country with Julie because we had only each other to turn to and spend time with. I even remember one night in June when I slept near the bay rather than going back to the house. Halfway through the night, I ended up at an exchange-program volunteer's house. I went to school the next day as though nothing had happened. The nice thing about southern Italy is that it doesn't get cold at night, so I could stand being down by the bay. But I could tell none of these things to my family or people outside the circle of the exchange program because it would look bad, and I had been advised that bad things happening in life doesn't mean anything. The best of course of action, I was advised, was to keep my mouth shut and do as I was told.

I learned very quickly to not respond to anything said to me, or at least to only speak when spoken to, and to spend as much time away from home as possible. I would always make sure that everything was clean before I left. I was usually the last one to leave in the mornings and the last one home. For the few dinners we had when other people came to dinner, I was expected to be there and put on a smiling face. It was in that moment that I realized you could completely despise people yet sit in the same room with them and have a somewhat good time. After some time, I had the chance to do my laundry, but I had to wash my clothes in the sink a few times. I was allowed to use the washing machine, but only when the family members weren't home. And don't forget that I was reminded I was a guest every other day.

I got a compliment from the family once; they said I could be worse. Most kids who come from split homes have a hard time in life, but I was reminded that whatever mind-numbing job I would get someday, I would think it could be worse. That was their version of condescending humor. I think it's interesting that a family that claimed to be so close while attacking me and critiquing my life today have very little contact with each other and are all spread out around Europe. Funny how life works, I guess. How strange it is to think back on how stupid I was to let myself be treated an any manner but with respect.

However, catholic guilt is a real thing, and I thought that somehow I was paying penance for some mortal sin I had committed. It's amazing how things would have been different if I had known then what I know now. I probably would have spoken up sooner. I would have been honest about everything that happened rather than just omitting the bad and keeping the good. Knowing now that there are not thousands of catholic saints waiting to keep me from heaven's gate simply because I didn't suffer enough makes me feel better. I have to remember that hurt people tend to hurt others. This family was never vetted and never wanted to be part of an exchange program, but since money was involved, it was hard for them to say no. They got what they needed—a story that they will tell about how they opened their home to a poor kid from Omaha. They can tell everyone how they shaped me into the person I am today and take credit for all the good things while denying the bad. Even twelve years later I still feel angered as to why they had to treat me bad just so they could feel better about themselves.

What great crime did I commit? I was the one who took the bigger risk by moving alone to a country I knew nothing about and learning a language that is in no way beneficial in my everyday life today. I took on all this turmoil—and for what? I would answer that question in a clichéd way by saying I did so to expand my life with more and better experiences, but how can I remember anything but the hatred I had for them in that moment in my life? Just thinking about their smug faces the last day I was there is unsettling. They told me I was always welcome and would always be part of their family as they each hugged me. I just cringed with anger in that moment. Why would I feel any differently if a family member or friend had done that here at home? So I guess it is my job to let go of their faults, as they never did to me. I should probably do what people do and just say, "Well, it was a different time and place, and if we could all go back, we would do it differently." One thing I will never let anyone take away from me is that I was good to them and turned the Catholic other cheek time and time again. So by being a good Catholic and seeing Pope John Paul II, I have officially filled my quota on my catholic checklist. The thing I had to keep in my mind was that every cloud has a silver lining; not being at the house very much gave me a lot of time to do and see many other things. So not everything was that terrible.

CHAPTER 6

Good Times and Italian Rhymes
(tempi buoni e rime italiane)

It is easy to paint a dark picture of drama and hurt feelings, but I experienced a lot of good times and funny moments. My personal favorite was, of course, Julie living up to her pretended ditzy blondeness. Just as in any language, there are Italian words that sound very similar but mean incredibly different things. One morning over coffee, Julie and I were talking and decided to get something to eat from the bakery in the back of the café. The mix-up that was about to occur was a simple case of mispronunciation. In Italy they have a chocolate- or sometimes fruit- or cream-filled crescent roll that is to die for, and this delicious treat is called a *Cornetto*, and that was the word that Julie was looking for when she went up to the counter to order. Instead she said the word "*Cornutta*," which, roughly translated, refers to a woman who is unaware she is being cheated on. ("*Cornutto*" is the male version of the same word). The barista, taken by surprise, told Julie she was sorry and that they did not sell cornutta, but that *i cornetti* had just come out of the oven and she had chocolate and vanilla. I have never in my life laughed so hard, and the barista forgive us foreigners and gave us two cornetti gratis.

When I wasn't on the road or hanging with Julie or Kristine, I had time to go on a lot of dates. It was while I was in Europe that I found out there is such a thing as a series of bad dates. All the girls I came across were amazing. (As a man, I have to say that, or I will never get laid again in life; all women are amazing and beautiful all the time, no matter what.) How do you not admire the female form? The problem is that most of those forms don't have a personality to go along with them. I remember my first date with an Italian girl, and all she wanted to do was to practice all of the English phrases she had learned in class; it was the most boring date I have ever been on to this day. Then she wanted to talk about all of her favorite American movies, television shows, and everything amazing about the great US of A. Thank the lord above she was completely gorgeous and a great kisser; otherwise, I would have faked an illness and gone home. After I realized I could kiss a girl and she wouldn't pull away, there was no need for talking anymore.

My second official date was actually the weekend of carnival, which is one of the greatest Fat Tuesday parties in the world—second only, I would assume, to Brazil's.

Southern Europeans take fat Tuesday very seriously. I got set up on a date with my host sister's friend, and we danced until about 3:00 a.m. on Ash Wednesday. The hardest part of that next day was having to get up early for church. (I think I have committed the sin of being hungover in church more while in Europe than during any other time of my life.) The music was great, and my host sister's friend being hot helped the night move from a Fat Tuesday party to a very romantic night. And thank God above that I could dance. I didn't realize how important dancing was to girls until I got all that relationship advice from all those southern European love gurus.

It wasn't just European and Italian girls that caught my attention. To this day I feel that the most gregarious and enticing people on the globe are from down under. The girls from Australia and New Zealand take partying and romance to levels never seen to many people. New Zealand girls are soft and kind and can party till the night's end, but Aussies are wild and beg to be tamed. (Okay, that was lame, but I am using poetic license here; I know that no girl needs to be tamed.) One of the best drinking contests I was ever in was with a girl from Sydney, and she beat everyone in the bar and got our whole tab paid for because the bartender was so impressed. The girls from South America were sassy and gorgeous, the Africans could dance and sing, the Asians were sweet and kind, and Russian girls were tempting, but I will forever tip my hat to the girls down under for teaching me how a man should be around a girl.

Not everything that I got to experience in Italy involved girls. One of my favorite memories is of the first time I went to local soccer match. There were wild crowds and chants, and the young and old were out in droves, being as wild as fans at any American football game I have been to. I can still hear the chants to this day. I was a little taken aback at first until I heard a child that could only have been about seven at the time get up and scream at the referee, using some of the most vulgar language around. All the nearby adults lifted the child up on their shoulders and cheered even more. It just goes to show you that you are never too young to start loving sports. I can still see a full stadium with beer all around as we taunted the other team with all our might, singing our chants and begging the other team's fans to have a better comeback. I had never been a huge fan of soccer, but there is something about being inside a stadium of thousands chanting in perfect unison. It is one of those experiences you have to experience to get a larger sense of community. And although the chants have faded from my memory, I can still faintly hear the crowd singing in the back of my mind. *Ole Taranto Ole!*

However, it's not just songs that cross my mind these days. One memory forever cemented in my brain is that of a couple stories a teacher told my senior class on the last day of school. One was a story about the creation of Italy. This was the last class I had before summertime fun began. It was about one o'clock in the afternoon, and it was hot and all the windows were open. The teacher finished saying good-bye to all the students, and then she started telling a story often told to Italian children. The teacher said she wanted us to feel like children one more time before school ended. It was a poignant moment; even though I had been with these people for only a few months, I too felt a sense of change because my time in high school was about to be over as well. As the teacher started the story, the room became completely silent as she sat there with joyful intent. The story goes as follows:

> Our story begins on God's eighth day. God looked at the world he had created, but something was still missing. God returned to his workshop to see what He had left over. After rummaging for several moments, he found a bag with all kinds of things inside it. Not knowing what do with these things, He found a pond in the center of the world and gently poured the contents of the bag into the pond. All the contents of the bag fell into the shape of a boot, and on the new strip of land there were mountains, deserts, valleys, and plains. Making sure that everything had

> left the bag, God shook the bag gently, and out came every animal, every person, and every plant known to man. The final specks of dust in the bottom of bag became stars in the sky above his new creation. As God looked down on this new creation, he saw that it sparkled very brightly. He could not believe that something that had not been intended was shining so brightly, almost as if the light coming from the center of the world were eternal. And that, my dear children, is why Italy is what it is today.

I will never forget that moment. That teacher gave us something that we didn't even know we needed—one last chance to be kids. Every time I think of that story, it makes me smile from ear to ear. Then she said, "Now I want to tell you one last story that was told to me, and I hope you pass it on yourself someday." The second story goes as follows:

> The Lord of the heavens and earth was sitting in heaven one day and called upon his three best angels. He said to them, "It has been many years since I have seen my people. I wish to send the three of you down to earth, and I wish you to experience everything mortal

life has to offer." The three angels did as they were instructed. They lived very well on earth, experiencing all humanity had to offer. After several years, the angels ascend to heaven to report the Lord Almighty. The Lord was very pleased with everything the angels had done. After listening to each angel, the Lord asked them all one question: "What was the hardest thing you ever had to do on earth?" The first angel said, "I believe the hardest thing to do is to say hello. Saying hello takes strength and bravery in a harsh world." The second angel said, "I believe the hardest thing is saying good-bye. Saying good-bye is painful, as you do not know if or when you will see someone again." Finally, the third angel said, "I think the hardest thing was to say 'I will see you again,' meaning it and making the effort to see that person again." Once again, the Lord was pleased with his angels. The Lord said to his angels, "I want you to always remember that with me, your Lord God, there is no hello or good-bye, but only 'We will see each other again.'"

The teacher then packed up all her things into her case, looked at the class, and said to us all, "Arrivaderci mia classe!" Then she walked out of the classroom, and we all went home feeling a little bit more grown up.

Two days later, my senior class had the biggest party I had ever been to down near the bay front. Halfway through the party that night, I found out from my school back in the States that I had passed all my classes and graduated high school. It was one amazing week. We spent the rest of the week having dinner out and giving gifts to each other.

CHAPTER 7

Time Flies By *(il tempo vola)*

As time drew to a close, I had traveled all over the mainland of Italy. I saw southern Austria, France, Switzerland and Slovenia. I had gotten to know people from all over the world. I had to attend several debriefing seminars about returning and what we had learned as exchange students. We were broken up in to regional groups. We stayed in a very nice hotel outside of Bari, the capitol of the province I was living in. There were about thirty students that attended my regional seminar. I could tell the huge difference in people from months earlier when we had all met in Rome. All the students seemed haggard and tired from there semester-long or yearlong stays. We had a lot of time to catch up with people we had known throughout our stays. We spent time talking in groups led by exchange-group leaders and advisers to see what was good, bad, or just needed changing. So much had happened, and there were so many thoughts running through my brain that I don't remember speaking up much. I spent a lot of time listening to some of the same problems we all faced. There were others who had raves for their families, schools, or communities. While I was listening, I couldn't help but think, *how did I get the placement I got?* Others seemed to have overcome or just ignored anything overtly bad, or were being dishonest, and others had just had great times. Was I thinking too much? Had I been unfair, possibly? Well, my youth and narcissism would not let me see what I see now. My pride had been damaged. I had been so good at so many things. I was so good with people, and I was frustrated at what kept this family and community from not seeing me for the good person I so aimed to be.

One night I couldn't sleep and was out in the courtyard of the hotel when a girl from Iceland that I had spent time with earlier in the year came out and sat next to me. She asked me why I couldn't sleep, and I told her that I felt so out of place at this seminar, listening to people's stories about triumph and growth, and that I didn't feel that I had grown at all. We talked for several hours that night; we walked down the road and went down the beach and back to the hotel. She kept telling me that to each should be his or her own and that no one's experience should be the same, as variety is the spice of life. It was easier to listen to clichés when we had some wine to help ease our stress. I was surprised that she had such a good way of putting things in perspective. After our long talk, we had a little more wine to toast our friendship, and then, after comforting me, she kissed me to reassure me that life would work out no matter what, because as long as we're alive, at least we're not dead. (To this day I don't what that means; I just agreed so I could kiss her again.)

After the seminar, the family I was living with actually warmed toward me a little. I think the fact that I was leaving really started to set in. Over that whole month, I had a chance to spend time with each of the five members of that family one-on-one. I got to hear some of their regrets, some of which were regarding me. I got a few semiapologies. For Italians, no matter how passionate they are about life, admitting they are wrong—even partially wrong—is like pulling teeth. I softened a little and allowed myself to sympathize with these people. How could I be completely mad when they had opened their home to me? I never thought that they were bad people or that things were never resolvable; I just wanted to have the same respect that I gave to them. I guess the one good thing about spending time with each one alone is that they seemed so docile—whereas while in a group, they were ravenous. As I listened to each of them over a few weeks' time, I came to realize that I had completely shut myself off to them. That part of their frustration came from trying to communicate with someone who just couldn't hear them. What I took to be abuse and disrespect was simply people not knowing how to communicate and just giving up. That is what we did together. We all gave up until it was almost too late. I guess it was a good thing to have a little emotion in the end to show that not everything was bad. It allowed us to look back on a few nice dinners, late-night talks, and shared stories from their lives and mine. I guess I was blinded by the fact that the people like Julie and Kristine, whom I had tried so hard to get to approve of me, made me miss out on a chance to get to know the people I was living with better.

I realize now my fault was not realizing there needed to be a balance between helping Julie and tending to the needs of my host family. It was so easy to have the friend to run to when life didn't turn out the way I wanted. I don't fault us for being the selfish teenagers we were, but now that time has passed. If I had one chance to go back, I would not shut myself off to people who wanted just one more minute of my time, even if at the time it was something that truly pained me.

During the last month I was in my town, Julie and I had a lot of time to talk. We would sit in a few different cafés and *gelaterias*. We talked about life, heartbreak, and what we were going to do without each other. I couldn't believe we had been through so much and then had to just say good-bye. We had laughed, cried, and fought like cats and dogs, as friends often do. How do you depart from someone who knows you better than anyone on the planet? The thing I will always truly respect about her is that no matter what moods we were in, or what was going on, we always talked and called each other; we never kept secrets or lied to each other. Everything was there, out in the open, judged simply as it was. To this day I am still so honored that I had her and Kristine to share in one of the greatest adventures of my life. Now that we are all older, we laugh at who we were, but we remember what we were to each other back then. We bonded as kids and stayed true to who we are. Bonding with people at that age, when you are not a kid but you are not an adult, is odd at first, but how could I have ever done any of the things I did—like travel, meet strangers, and take risks—without my two best gals. I am a better person today because of Julie and Kristine. I am forever in their debt for befriending me when they didn't need to but wanted to. Even after we parted, we still wrote and sent postcards. The other day I found one of those letters, and it sent my mind back to years ago. I felt for a brief moment like an eighteen-year-old kid trying to make sense of this crazy world.

One thing that I learned that struck me as odd when I first heard it, but now that I am older, it has more meaning. This is a phrase that means so much to Italians— "*ti voglio bene.*" It means "love for someone who is a good friend." It is never meant as romantic but as the ultimate respect for another person. One should be honored and take it as a great gift if someone says it back to you. So to all those people abroad who truly touched my life, let me say to you, *Gli voglio bene, e va via nella vita con fortuna.* (I love you all, and may your life have good luck.)

CHAPTER 8

The Triumphant Return *(ho tornato agli stati uniti dell'america)*

I had seen so much during my stay in Italy and Europe as a whole. So much had happened. I was there when Pope John Paul II reigned as king of Vatican City. I was in Europe during the fiftieth anniversary of Queen Elizabeth II's reign and the whole European party. I lived in Europe during the aftermath of September 11, 2001. I was among the last group of exchange students to live in Europe before the Euro was introduced as the main currency of the continent. I would stand in the bay and watch all the ships prepare to head to the Middle East to fight the first battle of the twenty-first century. It was a strange and wild time. Looking back, I can see all the amazing pieces of history I was a part of. At the time, it was just life; I guess that is why the old adage "We are living history" is really true. I saw ghettos and refugees, and I saw true poverty and societal prejudice like nothing I had seen in America, and somehow I came back prouder to be an American than I ever had been.

Even after everything I had seen and done, leaving was easier than I thought it would be. All the girls that were in my group were in tears with their families and friends that had shown up at the train station to say their good-byes to all of us. I gave my hugs and kissed both cheeks of a few dozen people as I loaded the train car we would all be staying in. With all the hugging and tears, the girls didn't realize the train was leaving. I was on the train, and they weren't. I heard the conductor say it was time to go, so I hopped off the train to get the girls, and then we just watched the train as it pulled away from the station with all our stuff. The train's staff was nice enough to drop our bags at the next station, and we had to wait for four hours at the train station for a new train to come take us to Rome. So we had a little extra time to say good-bye. Then Julie, Kristine, and I went to eat and hung out around downtown until our train to Rome arrived.

After the train came to pick us up, we had a very long trek back to Rome. We arrived just in time to get a sandwich, drink some beer, and go to bed so we could all get up early and leave for our home countries. The morning we all left, it was very hectic. There were students trying to get back to forty-five different countries. We were broken up into global groups. I was with all the people coming back to the United States and Canada. I had all of ten minutes to say good-bye to the rest of the people from all over the world who I knew. It wasn't until we left Rome and made it to Germany that we as a group realized that our stay was really over. I was so tired I just wanted to get on my next flight. Everyone in my group was completely sad and teary-eyed. I spent a good time in the Frankfurt airport comforting the people around me, telling them how great it would be to go back home and see our families and friends.

Things calmed down as we boarded our flights for New York. It was still early in the morning, so we could sleep until we got to New York. After about seven and a half hours, the pilot came over the intercom and said that we were approaching New York, and I could see the city in the distance as we passed by the Statue of Liberty. I had held everything together, but when we came over the horizon and I saw the giant hole in the Manhattan skyline, covered in dirt and snow, where months earlier the South Tower had been the standing, my heart sank and my eyes filled with tears. When we landed in New York, we headed in all different ways, and after a few good-byes, I got on my flight to California. I don't remember much about what happened after that, except that there was a group of Italians from Rome traveling to California for the first time; they asked me where in California they could see a real-life cowboy like one of those in all the spaghetti western movies they had grown up with. I don't remember having any advice about cowboys in California, but I do remember telling them I hoped they had a good time.

I arrived in Los Angeles and then went back to Eugene, Oregon. It was late at night by the time I got home, and after a few days I had readjusted to Oregon time. I had never realized how green Oregon actually was. For so many months, I had lived in a desert and that first winter back in the cold and rain was hard, but I'm an Oregonian now, so I love our winters and wouldn't change them for anything.

There was very little time to adjust, because just a few weeks after I returned home, my great-grandmother got very sick. I had just two more conversations with her, and then she left this world. So much change had happened, and I didn't even get to tell her about it.

This whole time I had not once cried—and I mean really cried—about everything that had happened. Then one night I went out for ice cream and to rent a movie. My mom called me and told me grandma had died, and I was fine. I told my dad I was going to take a drive and I would be back later. I stopped and got some ice cream and headed downtown. After I walked around town for about an hour, I went to the video store, and the clerk was so nice in helping me find something good to watch. (By the way, a video store is a store where we would get VHS tapes or DVDs; there was no online video streaming.) Just before I left, I saw a box set of *The Little Rascals*, and it didn't hit me until I got back into my car, but then I started bawling. My grandma Dolly and I had spent many times watching that old show, and since I was on the road, I had to pull over sobbing. Then I realized there was a police car behind me. He flashed his lights and came up to my car and asked how I was doing, and I was bawling like a baby. The only words I could get out were "I just got back into the country and found my grandma had died." What I didn't realize was that I was saying all this in Italian, completely confusing the officer. He kept asking me if I spoke English. Finally, I told him what was going on, and he asked if could step out of the car. We talked for a few minutes, and he told me to go get some coffee and sit somewhere. That officer was so great while listening to me completely unburden myself of everything that had happened to me that year. After I settled down, he told me life would only get better from then on. It had to, right? Then I got back into my car and started to laugh like a crazy person. So the officer who had watched me bawl in my car passed me and saw me laughing hysterically. I just thought to myself, *Why me?* I was wondering whether this was all just random or whether there was a purpose to it all.

CHAPTER 9

Was It an Accident or Meant to Be *(un incidente o voule essere)*

In the decade following my high school–endorsed exchange program, I often wondered what I missed my senior year. What about the school assemblies, dances, prom, and spending that final year with the people I grew up with? I know that world doesn't stop just because I can't see the whole world at once. I wonder if I have gotten to the places I've been, had the chances I've had, or met the people I know because of my experience. Was the growth that happened real or just one of things I talk about to make people think I am different?

I have had way over a decade to try to answer that question of "meant to be, or accident?" My answer is this: life is a series of choices. I may not be an overall better person in life because of my experience, but living outside the United States has given me the chance to see my homeland for what it is—a great place filled with opportunity and growth in life. Living abroad made me realize how lucky I am to be in a place where dreams and visions do come true. Has my life worked out in any form of the word "perfectly"? That is a big N-O, but I am now more accepting of people and other cultures. I have more sympathy but very little empathy. Empathy can sometimes be substituted for pity, and I don't pity people who have had similar life paths; I simply look at what they have to work with, and if I can help, I do.

In the years following my exchange, I was part of an Italian club in college, I did language tutoring and paper editing for years, and although I still haven't found where my place is in life, talking to people about my experiences has been great. It has allowed me to be more open about so many things in my life.

Finally, there was onemore thing I had to do to close the chapter on that piece of my life. It was something that took me ten years to actually do for my own soul's healing and freedom. In the summer of 2012, when I went back to Omaha to see my newborn niece, I went back to the cemetery where my great-grandparents are buried, and I did something I should have done long ago. I told the two people I cared for the most what had happened on my trip to Italy all those years ago. Although they didn't talk back and it was just me standing and talking to a headstone, for some reason it was freeing for me, and I'm glad I did it. I couldn't believe that was the thing that healed me from all those year ago. After I told them everything, I wished them good-bye and I got teary-eyed. Then I remembered not to say "Good-bye" but just "See you again soon." So I walked back to their headstone, and I gently kissed my hand and placed it on the stone and said, "I love you guys, and I will see you again soon."

I walked away that day in 2012 a changed person. All that had happened finally felt like it had come full circle and was meant for a greater purpose in my own life. I am forever grateful for everything that happened and everyone who made it possible for me go live way far from home and do what so many more people should get the experience of doing. I may be older, and my hair is grayer now, but I still dream of those beaches and those three teenagers without a care in world cruising along the bay laughing, singing, and joking about the times we lived, the times we died, and those moments when we found life again.

I have been trying to think of the best way to completely end this chapter in my life, and there is only one way I can do so. Alfred Lord Tennyson (1809–1892) wrote one of the greatest poems ever written in 1833—"Ulysses." (Seriously, go to a library or go online and read it.) It is one of the most over quoted poems and is usually the first mentioned when talking about Tennyson, but it is the end of this poem that truly strikes me to the core. It is a poem about a man who went on a long adventure, and now that he is older, he is contemplating taking another life adventure.

To sail beyond the sunset, and the baths
Of all the western stars, until I die.
It may be that the gulfs will wash us down:
It may be we shall touch the Happy Isles,
And see the great Achilles, whom we knew
Though much is taken, much abides; and though
We are not now that strength which in old days
Moved earth and heaven; that which we are, we are;
One equal temper of heroic hearts,
Made weak by time and fate, but strong in will
To strive, to seek, to find, and not to yield.

Throughout my life I have had a series of adventures. What the poem says to me is that we must never stop with our adventures. There are more skies to see, and one day we might get to that place of comfort and contentment—but why rush when the world has so much to offer? And although I had more carefree whims long ago, there is still a part of me that is proud I proved to myself that a challenge could be met, the risks could be conquered, and love could be found. That is what I learned from my story, and it was the lesson I missed that I was so worried about; everyone and everything else was filler. Not that people, places, and time didn't matter; they mattered in the moment, but the universe wanted me to gather more from my experience than a full list of contacts and a passport full of stamps. I live each day to the fullest, as the old cliché states, and I have learned that an old dog *can* learn new tricks and that it is good to have loved even if no one loved me in return.

Now, I know my words are not as profound as those of someone as great as Alfred Lord Tennyson, but this was my story, told my way. Most of it was boring and mundane, some of it was exciting, and some was history making. A story that has spent over a decade in my heart—buried under regret, shame, and pride—has now been told. Take from it what you must, or take nothing at all.

For my next chapter in life, I will take Tennyson's advice to strive for better—not just for me but also for others around me—to seek for things yet to be found and the secrets the world holds, to find others as well as myself, and to never stop no matter what happens until the sun sets on my life and, as stated in the Oscar-winning movie *The Lion King*, I will return to the stars where all kings do. (That's funny, because my last name is King.)

It all seems like a great story still rolling around in my head, but I know deep down inside there was a young guy long ago who threw caution to the wind and flew over continents and an ocean to find himself and to return a better, well-rounded man who, despite himself, still is an adventurer at heart.

So I say to you all thank you. May peace and love find you and never say good-bye but always see you again.

Interlude

Since this story helped to shape the person I am today, I feel that in true Jessy King fashion, I can't just leave the reader with one more piece of me; I need to give a something extra. Years ago I wrote a short story inspired by my Italian trip. I could not think of any better way to end my semiautobiographical opinion piece, and that is a fancy way to say "my book," than with one of my classically crafted Jessy King–style stories.

Please enjoy "Three Days in Venice: The James Starker Story."

II

Three Days in Venice

Prologue
Hello, My Name Is James

Have you ever wanted to get away—to try to escape? Well, I do that quite a lot. Every year I make sure that no matter what, I stay for three days in Venice, Italy. You might ask, why Venice? Why Italy? Well, the answer is adventurous romantic chaos—one simple phrase that makes life worthwhile. See, we all wish for adventure, romance, and a little chaos; we just want them in our own place and time, and under our control. I, like most people, was under the impression that as long as I kept to myself and was quiet, no adventurous romantic chaos would happen to me. Life, on the other hand, had a completely different avenue I was to go down.

CHAPTER 1

A Long Train Ride

Part 1: Shall We Exchange Names?

As I boarded the train, I noticed that there was only one other person in my cabin. It was a very attractive young lady, blonde as blonde could be. Her hair color gave away simply that she was not an Italian native. The train attendant came through the cabin asking for tickets, in the most hurried of manners. As I sat down, I couldn't help but notice that the young lady was looking at me. Secretly smiling to myself, I simply sat in the nearest seat to the door of cabin. The train started to pull out of the station, and the young lady got up, walked over, and sat in the seat directly across from me. Not knowing what to say at first, I decided to say the first thing that came to mind.

"Hello."

"Hello," she replied with an accent I couldn't recognize. "How are you today?"

"I am doing well; I have a long trip ahead of me. I am glad you are here; maybe you can break some of my boredom."

"May I ask your name?"

"I am Ana Devaroux. And you are?"

"I am James Starker."

"So, Mr. Starker, where are you headed?"

"I am going to Venice for a long weekend. And where are you headed?"

"What a wonderful coincidence; I have business in Venice. It is one of my favorite places to visit, so I usually stay a few days after work just to wander around the city."

"I hope this is not inappropriate, but I love your accent; where are you from?"

"I am French Canadian, but I went to boarding schools all over Europe. And where are you from, Mr. Starker?"

"I am from Hollywood."

"Wow, Hollywood—land of actors, musicians, and the super wealthy. Has any of that Hollywood magic worn off on you?"

"No. I was recently fired from a television show writing team for being too predictable. My boss told me that my mundane life had trickled into my writing and that until I had a more interesting life, or ideas to bring to the table, I was out of job. So I decided that I this was a perfect time to go to Venice and just get away from my life, even if it is just for a weekend."

"Well, you may be a predictable man, but you sure know how to start conversations with strangers." With the most infectious giggle, she crossed her legs and shone a beautiful smile. "Shall we order something to eat, since we both have a long trip ahead of us?"

"I think that would be great; I'm starving."

Part 2: Connection on a High-Speed Rail

After a great conversation, good food, and wonderful company, we agreed it was time for some shut-eye. As Ana fell asleep, I couldn't help but stare at this amazingly beautiful and intelligent lady. A thousand thoughts were running through my brain. There was no way I would be able to sleep. As I closed my eyes, I replayed this wonderful evening over and over in my head, smiling at all the witty and charming things I had said to make Ana smile, laugh, and giggle. I ran through every laugh line, wrinkle of her nose, and every time we had made eye contact, and then I finally fell asleep.

CHAPTER 2

Venice, You Never Cease to Amaze Me

Part 1: Leaving the Train

As I woke up from what seemed like a yearlong slumber, I noticed my late-night dinner date had left already. However, she had left a small note with her name, what seemed like the name of a hotel, and a phone number on it. I wasn't able to look at it very long before a train attendant began escorting people off the train as if it were a matter of life and death. I stepped off the train with my bag and took one more glance at the little note. I found my driver, who led me to the car and took to my hotel. When I arrived at the hotel, I realized it was the same hotel as the one Ana had written the name of in her note. As I was checking in, I had to ask the hotel desk clerk about her.

"Excuse me, but I was wondering if a friend of mine is staying here?"

In a thick Italian accent, the clerk replied, "What is the name of your friend, Signore Starker?"

"Her name is Ana Devaroux."

"Yes, Signorina Devaroux is in room 212. Would you like to me to tell her you are here?"

"No, thank you; I just wanted to know if she checked in."

"Well, everything is in order, Signore. Here is your room key, and as per your request, there will be a car to pick you up for dinner at La Café de Mare."

"Thank you."

As I turned around to walk to the elevator, I heard a familiar giggle, and who was it but Ana, dressed as if she were a Hollywood actress. As I walked through the lobby toward the elevator, our eyes met and she gave me a smile. She excused herself from her conversation to come over to me.

"Hey, are you stalking me?" she asked with a giggle.

"I was beginning to think the same thing about you."

"Well, this meeting I have shouldn't take long. When I'm done, we should grab lunch."

"Sure. Just come to my room when you're done, and we'll make a plan. I'm in the presidential suite on the top floor."

"Wow, a suite," Ana said, half impressed and sarcastically.

As she walked away, I couldn't help but stare, and I

ended up missing the elevator and decided just to take the stairs. Not being able to get this young woman out of my mind was throwing my usually organized thoughts into chaos. This trip to Venice had been a tradition of mine for a while; I was conflicted about letting this girl interrupt my predictable life. Then, with the thought of predictability, I thought about losing my job and everything else my predictable life had made me lose. So I decided that I would throw caution to the wind, let go of tradition, and dive into romantic chaos.

Part 2: Short Silence

As I took a look around my suite, I put my things on the king-size bed and proceeded to the bathroom. It was a beautiful bathroom with a huge tub and a window that looked out over the city. I decided to take a warm bath and look out on the city to wash away the feeling of a long train ride. I hoped to have thoughts of good Italian food and a relaxing weekend.

After a great bath, I changed into comfortable lunch attire, opened my laptop, logged on to the Internet, and looked to see what kind of gossip I could find about Hollywood since I had been fired. It was disgusting. The studio head, who had fired me, was now receiving some sort of award for his progressive risks he had taken in television and movies—risks that he had told me personally he was against. But that is the great thing about Hollywood—it doesn't matter what you have actually done; as long as you are in the right place to claim any fame, that is all people care about.

Just then I heard a knock at the door, so I closed my laptop, walked over to the door, and opened it to find Ana.

"Hey, are you ready for lunch?" she asked.

"Yes. Where should we go?"

"Let's just walk around and find something; then let's go to Saint Mark's Cathedral."

"Let me just call for a car."

"A car? Man, you really are from California. We are going to walk like normal people."

CHAPTER 3

Saint Mark's

Part 1: Art and Food

After a quick lunch, Ana and I walked through Saint Mark's Cathedral, taking in all the art and history. I noticed that Ana kept checking her cell phone, as if some sort of eminent emergency were soon to fall upon us. She kept looking around as if we were being followed.

"Hey, are you okay?" I asked.

"I'm fine," Ana said very curtly.

"You have seemed distracted all day long."

"I've just got a lot of work to do when we get back to the hotel."

"Should we just go?"

"I'll tell you what—I will just meet you for dinner later tonight."

Part 2: A Dinner to Remember

I would have assumed Ana's behavior to be strange, but ever since I had met her, nothing had seemed normal. I went about my day and slowly made my way back to the hotel. I then changed into my favorite suit and made my way back to the hotel lobby, where the girl that had seemed so distressed and preoccupied now seemed to be relaxed. She was incredibly well dressed in a little black dress that left nothing to the imagination. Seeing her looking so beautiful and relaxed made me forget about her odd behavior earlier that day.

"Ana," I said, "You look amazing."

"Oh, how sweet of you to say; you look very handsome yourself."

"Are you ready for dinner? The car is outside."

"I think a car is a bad idea. Why don't you let me drive?"

"Okay," I said suspiciously.

The two of us got into her Mercedes, and she drove directly to the café. It was one of those rides in the car that was quiet except for small talk. It was starting to bother me a little that whenever I offered to do something or go somewhere, her relaxed demeanor changed. It was as if she were hiding something sinister or nefarious.

We arrived at the restaurant, the valet took her car, and we walked in and headed for a private table in the back.

As we sat down, our server brought us complimentary Champagne. This whole evening just seemed too overly rehearsed, almost as if we were on a movie set. I couldn't hold my tongue anymore; I had to say something to Ana.

"Ana, what is going on? You have been acting completely strange ever since I met you yesterday. I understand that we are strangers, but still, you have to tell me what is going on."

"It is really hard to explain."

"We are not leaving here until I hear what is going on."

"Okay, look, we are not strangers; I actually work at the studio that you just got fired from. Frank Conley is my boss. You have no idea what is actually going on or why you were really fired."

"So then just tell me!"

"Frank is being investigated for money laundering and drug smuggling from Mexico; he is using his TV studio as a cover. Well, someone leaked where the money and drugs were coming from. The police have leads at the studio but no names. So Frank fired you and is preparing frame you so he can save himself."

"So how do you fit into all this?" I asked.

"Here is where the plan gets weird. Frank sent me here to Italy to kill you so you wouldn't be able to testify against him if they somehow connected him to the drugs, but you were the only man at the studio that was nice to me. You treated me like a person, not just some silly intern or eye candy. So I lied to Frank so I could come on this trip and warn you."

"I have no idea what to say. This is the most bizarre thing I have ever heard. I knew Frank hated me and was trying to get rid of me, but I thought it was because the studio wanted to replace Frank with me. I had no idea he was a criminal. How long have you known about this?"

"I found out about a month ago."

"Why didn't you say something sooner?"

"Frank wouldn't let me and told me he would kill me if I slipped up at all."

"So what do we do now?"

"Let's just eat and pretend nothing is going on. I have no idea if I'm the only person Frank sent over. If we act like we know anything, we could alarm one of Frank's goons."

"What do you mean 'Frank's goons'?"

"I keep getting text messages that say eyes are watching me and I'd better get on with killing you or else something bad is going to happen to both of us."

As I was unable to absorb any of this, dinner was mostly quiet, and so was the reluctant car ride back to the hotel. We got back to hotel, and the chaos continued. The desk clerk said they had changed rooms for me because of a bomb threat in the presidential suite while I was out. I protested about staying in any room in that hotel, but I ended up just staying in Ana's hotel room because she was convinced we were more protected staying in the same place versus trying to find someplace new, opening ourselves up to possible attacks. As I lay in bed, I couldn't believe all this was happening; it was as if the movies had become real life. I remembered writing things like this, but I never thought hired hits, money laundering, drugs, and lies were part of the real lives of boring, predictable people like me. I had barely been in Italy twenty-four hours, and I had already met a crazy lady and lost my hotel room and a chance for three days of relaxation.

CHAPTER 4

Early to Rise

Part 1: Run, James, Run

I woke up to the buzzing of a cell phone on the table next to my bed. Ana jumped up and grabbed it.

"James, we have to go! The men in the car across the street—they are gone. The desk clerk just messaged me."

I jumped out of bed, put on my jacket and grabbed my bag, and we left the room and headed for the service elevator in the back of the building. We got in the elevator with a hotel attendant that was waiting for us. We exited the elevator to find a black car waiting for us in the back alley, so we got in and the car sped off. We pulled out onto a main road, and four other black cars appeared and started to gain on us. The closest car rammed the side of our car, and we sped up to try to lose them, but all that did was make them chase us more. We got onto what seemed like an Italian highway, and we headed out of Venice.

"Where are we going?" I asked.

"We are going to little town called Gorizia, where we can stock up on supplies and get a better grasp as to what is going on."

"So I take it that since you have not killed me yet, Frank wants you dead too."

"I guess."

"You *guess?* This is ludicrous. Ana, we need to go to the police."

"We can't. All that would do is bring attention to us that we don't need. All we have to do is fake our deaths and we can get away."

"Oh, so we just fake our deaths; why didn't I think of that? Oh yeah, because no one normal ever does that. And we can't just try to outrun these guys; all they are going to do is keep following us."

"I know."

Ana reached into her bag and pulled out a number of what looked like grenades.

"What are those?" I asked.

"Smoke bombs, to cover what we are going to do."

"What are we … never mind."

Ana rolled down the window and threw out six of the smoke bombs, which happened to be all different colors. The black cars disappeared into the smoke, giving us time to get to a side street, where we parked and caught our breath.

Part 2: Chasing Danger

I was trying to make sense of what was happening, and not understanding one piece of it.

"James, do you know how to shoot?" Ana asked me.

"Shoot what?"

"A gun? Do you know how to shoot a gun?"

"No!"

"Well, here is what you are going to do; you are going to point and shoot!"

She handed me a semiautomatic handgun. She then pulled out from the side street and started to chase the cars and men who had been chasing us. I had no idea why we weren't just going the other way. The drivers seemed to be driving as if they were in some Hollywood-style chase scene. My heart was racing one hundred miles a minute. My hands were shaking. I could barely hold on to the gun. Ana was preparing for what looked like an all-out spaghetti western brawl. As the car's speed exceeded one hundred miles an hour, the black cars became visible.

"James," Ana said, "roll down your window. As we get closer, get ready to open fire. And don't stop shooting no matter what."

She handed three magazines for my handgun. The

tension in the moment was completely indescribable, and I felt as if I were dreaming all of this. Then, seemingly in slow motion, I saw Ana pull the trigger, and I heard loud bangs as each bullet left her gun.

CHAPTER 5

Time for a Firefight

Part 1: From Frozen to Action Star

As I watched bullets fly from the black cars and from our car and heard the constant popping sounds, as if a firework had been set ablaze, I finally got my wits about me and joined the chaos. The four black cars screeched to a halt, and all four formed a blockade on what looked like a highway bridge. The men got out of their cars, switched from handguns to assault weapons, and began peppering our vehicle like nothing I had ever seen. Ana turned our car and presented it broadside, and we climbed to the other side, using the car for cover. To this day, I don't know how a single bullet never hit us. Ana and the four men exchanged methodical fire from both sides of the bridge. Then the shooting just stopped, apparently for no reason at all. I heard mumbled words from the other side of the bridge, and I turned to see what Ana was doing.

"What are we going to do?" I asked.

"Run!" Ana replied.

"What? Run? I am tired of all of this. I am done. Someone is going die. I'd rather it be now than later."

I stupidly decided to stand up, at which point I saw the four men point their guns at me.

"*Who do you work for?*" I shouted. "Tell me who you work for, now! I am tired of being chased! All I wanted was a quiet vacation from my life, which has upside down since I lost the only job I have ever known in my life. All I wanted was a break to clear my head. *Someone say something!*"

"Throw your gun over the side of the bridge and maybe we can talk!" replied one of the gunmen in an Italian accent.

I slowly backed up to the side of the bridge, held the gun in the air, and dropped it over the side to show them that I was following their instructions. As I stood there waiting for the next move, I watched as all four gunmen put new magazines in their assault rifles. Then all four men opened fire on me. It felt as if I were being stung by bees, and I felt myself falling backward over the side of the bridge. I couldn't catch my breath. I couldn't feel anything except the sensation of falling, and as I looked up, all I saw was the side of bridge getting farther and farther away from me. Then I hit the water with a thud and slowly sank to bottom of the river. I was feeling death come over me; then I blacked out.

Part 2: Meanwhile, on the Bridge

The four men got back in their cars and drove away, leaving a screaming and crying Ana looking down at the water. Ana was in complete disbelief. The man she had been sent to kill, and instead tried to save, had fallen to his death, and there was nothing she could do about it. She screamed for help and then ran back to her car and tried to find a phone to call for help. After about a half an hour, some local police showed up. Ana tried to explain what had happened to police in very broken Italian. The investigators looked up and down the river, but no body was recovered. The police took Ana to the hospital to make sure she was okay. Ana was in complete disbelief as to what she had witnessed, but she knew she still had a phone call to make.

She dialed a number, and Frank Conley soon answered.

"Hello."

In complete sadness, Ana said, "It's done."

"Okay, when are you coming back to LA?"

"I can't, because I am part of an investigation now. Four Italian hit men made a huge mess when they shot and killed James."

"What?"

"Yeah, I never got a chance to kill him, and the Italian authorities can't find James's body, and I can't leave the country until they find him."

"What?"

"Stop saying 'what,' Frank! Do you understand what kind of attention this is going to bring to us if they find out what really happened? Do you know what they are going to do me?"

"Just sit tight. Don't talk to anyone until one of my attorney friends gets there. I will be out on the next flight for Italy. I will be there tomorrow. Just don't say anything."

Part 3: And the Interrogation Begins

The next day, an investigator came to speak with Ana at the hotel and everyone who had encountered her. After what seemed like a daylong question-and-answer session, by some miracle Frank showed up two hours ahead of schedule. Frank walked over to Ana, who was sitting on a couch in the hotel lobby.

"Ana, how are you doing?" he asked.

"Oh, I'm great! I have had so much fun in Italy."

"We don't need sarcasm."

"I am trying really hard to understand everything that has happened. You told me this was easy. You told me we could get rid of James and we could frame the recently deceased and then we would live the rest of our days in Hawaii, but you want to know what is going to happen to me? I am going to prison, and after they arrest me, I am ratting you out. I am telling them everything."

"Just be calm. I have the best attorney in the world. Just be patient, and everything will work out."

CHAPTER 6

Frank the Con Artist

Part 1: The Master at Work

Ana could not believe how masterful and in control Frank was. Frank spoke beautiful Italian and explained a fantastical story of how James Starker was a very bad man. He told the investigators about how James had enemies everywhere and was the drug king of California. Frank also described the ruthlessness of James and told them that he had kidnapped Ana and used her as cover so he could try to escape but at last was taken out, and that the world was much better off without James Starker.

Frank was so convincing that the police closed the case, and since there was no evidence connecting him or Ana to any nefariousness, they were free to leave the country. Ana was just glad everything was over. It had been one of the worst days of her life, and Ana could never look at Venice the same. She could not get out of her mind that if it hadn't been for her, James Starker would still be alive. Frank, however, was as happy as he could be. His nemesis was dead. He had blamed all the strange activity at his movie studio on a dead guy, and he and Ana could live happily ever after in Hawaii.

Ana and Frank took a train from Venice back to Milan so they could catch their flight out of Italy and put all this drama behind them. Frank would not for one-minute give Ana the chance to talk about anything that had happened over the last three days.

"You need to act happier," Frank said on the train.

"What?"

"Look, what's done is done. You didn't do anything wrong, and you didn't have to kill anyone. No need to be sad at all. When we get back to LA, let's pack a couple of bags, go to Hawaii, and relax like we had always planned."

"Fine, whatever. Can we just not talk? I'm kind of tired."

"Listen, you knew what you were getting into when we started all this. James was in the way. He was starting to find things out, and it was only a matter of time before he found out what we had been doing and went to the police and sent the both of us to prison forever. Just think of our future. Let's once and for all put this behind us."

The rest of the train ride from Venice to Milan was filled with awkward silence. Frank decided to break the silence by mingling with the other passengers. Ana just glared at Frank; she could not believe that she had allowed herself to ever like him at all. Even though she knew that she hadn't killed James, she felt guilty that she hadn't done more to try to save him. She didn't know how she was going to live with that guilt, but she knew that she did not want to have any contact with Frank after they got back to LA.

Part 2: Flight Home

After what seemed like an eternity, Ana and Frank made it back Los Angeles. Frank hailed Ana a cab.

"Hey, you should go home and rest," he said to her. "I'll come by later with some dinner, and we can plan our trip to Hawaii."

"Okay."

"And remember: we've got nothing but good things in store for us."

CHAPTER 7

Someone Found a Body

Part 1: This Never Happens in Real Life ... Does It?

Frank is working in his office when the four hired hit men show up.

"What are you guys doing here?" Frank asks.

One of the men says, "We just saw on the news that an unidentified body was found in a little village south of Venice."

"What? The police looked for days and found nothing. It doesn't matter; that body could be anyone's."

"No, it's James. Here is the news article." He opened up his laptop to show the Italian video of the police retrieving a body from the river. "And now it's made it to the national news in Italy. It's only a matter of time before the BBC and CNN pick up the story. Everything is over, and we all decided to visit you to make sure that our names won't somehow come up.

"You guys never told me your names. You simply called yourselves the Stefano brothers."

"Well, just to let you know, until this whole thing blows over, we're going to keep an eye on you to make sure you don't do anything stupid."

"Stupid?"

"You know, so you don't accidently change your story and let it slip out that we were the ones that killed James, and to make sure you don't give any information to the police about what we look like or sound like—or even how you found us."

The four men left Frank's office, leaving Frank noticeably shaken. He got up from his desk, left all his work, and went out to the parking lot and got into his car. He drove over to Ana's apartment, ran up to her door, and frantically knocked. There was no answer. He took a credit card out of his wallet and slipped it between the door and its frame and let himself into her apartment. He noticed that it had been ransacked. Just then his cell phone rang. Startled, he quickly pulled it out of his pocket and answered it.

"Hello?"

The hit man who had spoken to Frank earlier replied, "If you are looking for Ana, we took her as an insurance policy to make sure you will do exactly what we want you to do."

"Oh, God, please doesn't hurt her."

"No harm will come to her as long as you meet us at the abandoned studio behind 20th Century Fox. Be there at six p.m., and come alone—no police, no cell phones, just you."

"Okay, just please, please don't do anything to her."

Then the phone went dead. Frank got into his car and started to drive over to the studio.

Part 2: Who Knew Frank Could Get Scared?

Frank made it to the old abandoned studio. He walked in and realized that there was a table in the middle of the dark, drafty, and dilapidated building. The table was under an old spotlight that flickered every time a breeze came through the studio. Since he had left his phone in the car, he didn't know the exact time, but he knew he was early. He looked around the studio and saw ratty old posters on the walls and parts of sets that were rotting and falling apart. He had a million thoughts running through his head about what he had gotten himself and Ana into. He just kept hoping that nothing would happen to her.

Then two of the hit men arrived.

"I'm glad you decided to show up," said the hit man who always did the talking. "You know, I hate people like you, Frank—thinking you can get away with everything. You told us that the girl would take care of everything and that the only thing we had to do was make sure that there was no body, no evidence, and no more James Starker. And your girl interfered with that plan. She actively tried to save him. All we wanted to do was our job. Then it dawned on us after we left Italy that if you were so good at framing James, why wouldn't we be next? I mean, Frank, you work in the movies, and you are the type of person who hates loose ends.

"No, no, I would have never said anything about you guys."

"Frank, if we thought for a second that could be true, we would not have kidnapped your girlfriend. We just wanted to talk to you to make sure that you know who is in charge now. And your silence must be secured. So what I and my brothers are going to do is set times when we check in with each other once in a while."

"Okay, anything you want."

"And at these little visits, we are going to collect some of that drug money you have been laundering. You know—keep us from going to police."

"Seriously, I will do whatever you want as long as I get Ana back safe."

The hit man who had been speaking walked over to the other hit man and whispered something to him, and then he left. When the second hit man returned, he had Ana and the other two hit men with him. The men set Ana in a chair next to the table and found another chair for Frank to sit in. After both of them were seated, the men tied them both to the chairs, and then they walked a few feet away and started talking in a huddle.

Frank looked at Ana. "We are going to get out of here, and everything will be fine; I promise."

"Shut up, Frank; everything that has happened has been the opposite of what you have promised would happen. I am done with you and all your stupid promises."

"Listen, if we don't cooperate with them, they are going to turn us in to the police—or worse, they will kill us."

"I'm done, Frank. You do whatever it is you need to do, but if prison is the only way to get away from all this, then I am prepared to spend the rest of my days there."

The four men walked over to Frank and Ana.

"Okay," said the chief hit man. "We have decided that will take 49 percent of all the money you bring in on your drug game. As for the girl, well, she needs a job where we can keep in an eye on her and make sure that her guilt doesn't get the best of her and cause her to run to the police, so we will find her a job with us."

"Okay," said Frank.

"Frank, man, you have got to loosen up. We are giving you a good deal here. With us around, you have protection for you and your girl, you have business partners to make sure you are not getting ripped off on the black market, and of course you have the freedom of knowing you will never get caught. So now I'm going to get some food while my brothers stay here with you guys. Then we can finish our little meeting, and then everyone can go home happy.

The hit man walked away while the other three stood guard.

CHAPTER 8

The Twist

As the chief hit man returned, everyone was silent. He threw on the table what looked like sub-style sandwiches. He untied Frank and Ana and pushed a sandwich in front of each them. Frank and Ana reluctantly started eating; neither of them wanted to do anything to upset the temporary kidnappers. The hit man then threw a sandwich to each of the other guys and told them to start eating. Then a slamming door in the back of the studio broke the silence.

"Boys, go check it out!" the chief hit man said.

The three other men jumped up, guns drawn, and slowly moved to the back of the studio. They made their way to the back door and carefully slipped out the back, realizing there was nothing outside. Then the door opened again, slowly. The three men walked back in, except they had no weapons and were holding their hands in the air. Frank, Ana, and the chief hit man heard someone say, "Keep moving!"

The dark, shadowy man made the three hit men walk to the edge of where the shadows met the flickering light of stage lamp. The muffled voice said, "On your knees!"

The men got on their knees, and the shadowy man walked behind each of them and knocked them out with the butt of the rifle he was holding. The three men fell to ground. The shadowy man then looked at the remaining hit man and told him to sit next to the Frank and Ana at the table, and he then told everyone at the table to look down at the table and not move their heads unless they were spoken to. Then the shadowy figure walked into the light and took off a black bandanna that was covering his mouth and nose. Ana could not help herself and looked up at the man, even though he had told everyone at the table not to do so. Ana realized it was James. He was not dead after all. *How could this be?* she thought. *I saw him get shot and fall to his death off that bridge!*

"Well, well, well," said James. "What a sorry, sad group this is. Frank, dude, why did you think you could just kill me and blame all your bad dealings on me? You publicly fired me, and there was no way in hell the media wasn't going to be all over me. And you are such a glory hog; you are always in the news. Someone was bound to dig up what you have been doing. Ana, girl, I knew you looked familiar, and your French Canadian accent sucks. You are from Kennebunkport, Maine. While I was dead, I had some time to figure out who you really are. Oh, and by the way, the other reason I knew you weren't French Canadian is that when you first said 'Toronto,' you pronounced the second *t*. Canadians—especially French Canadians—don't do that. You need to work on that if you ever decide to get back into acting. And you over there—the muscle with the gun—I would like you tell these two sleaze balls who you really are."

The hit man, still looking at the table, said, "I am special agent Allan Green from the FBI. Frank, we have been following you for a while now, but we could never get close enough to get hard evidence. So when you fired James here, we approached him before he took off for Venice and told him we wanted to use him as bait to catch you and get a confession out of you."

"Hey, Frank, one more thing," said James. "Let me give you a little advice from one man to another. Sometimes in life we all need adventurous romantic chaos, and other times we just want to take our formers boss's money while he is sent to prison. And if you ever make it back to Venice, give me a call, and let's do this again sometime!"

About the Author

Jessy King was born in South Omaha, Nebraska, and given the name Jesse Enrique Mata. After attending a private grade school in Omaha, Jessy moved to Oregon, where he attended three years of high school before spending his last year of high school in Europe. After he returned from Europe, he attended Oregon State University. Shortly thereafter, he had his very first song produced and became a published lyricist, and this is where his love of writing began. Over the next decade, Jessy King did small projects and participated in onstage and street plays until, close to a decade later, in late 2012, his first play was picked up by private investors and became his first street theatre play to be adapted into book form. Jessy King continues to write books, plays, poems, and music, and he still resides in Oregon.